I0173437

Dad Was Taken
to
Watch a Lynching

Occasional Poems

Richard Baldwin Cook

Dad Was Taken
to
Watch a Lynching

Occasional Poems

First Edition 2014

Copyright Richard Baldwin Cook
ISBN 978-1-935538-07-3

Nativabooks.com
Nativa LLC
Cockeysville, MD

Available at bookstores
and at Lulu.com, Amazon.com,
Google ebooks, etc.

Other books by Richard Baldwin Cook include:

Splendid Lives and Otherwise
That's What I'm Talking About
All of the Above I
All of the Above II

ACKNOWLEDGEMENTS

These poems (some, revised) first appeared in the following *on line* publications:

Dad Was Taken to Watch a Lynching - *Pen in Hand,* Summer, 2013, v 26, n 3
Good Robert Coles - *Farm Worker Documentation Project*
I Like the GPS - *Syndic Journal No 7*
Today is Election Day - *Pen in Hand,* Winter 2013 v 26, n 1
Milton Visits the Condemned Galileo - *Pen in Hand,* Winter 2013 v 26, n 1
Ripped Messiah - *Syndic Journal No 7*
Short Order - *Pen in Hand,* Winter 2013 v 26, n 1
Simulacra - *Syndic Journal No 6*
Te Mataron, David - *Por* Que? also
David - Why Did They Murder You? - *Pen in Hand,* Winter 2012, v 25, n 4

The reader of the Spanish language poems is the beneficiary of editorial ministrations extended by Lilliana Mendez Villareal, for which the writer is grateful.

Back cover photo of the writer: photographer unknown; professional highlights made by William Dorland Cook Sr. Thanks, Bill.

STRONGER LESSONS

Have you learn'd lessons only of those who
admired you?

and were tender with you, and stood
aside for you?

Have you not learn'd great lessons from those who
reject you,
and
brace themselves against you
or
who treat you with contempt
or
dispute the passage with you?

Walt Whitman
Sands at Seventy
Leaves of Grass

CONTENTS

Dad Was Taken to Watch a Lynching

Dad Was Taken to Watch a Lynching
He was seven, maybe a little older, little younger.
I was a boy when . . . wait a minute . . .
Did he tell me this? Did I overhear?
An echo in the darkening wind tunnel of memory?

His father, his grandfather, was a preacher
a Man of the Gospel.
Was it Albany? Danville? Farmville? Charlottesville?
Pick-a-ville . . .Towns where his Pa preached
against liquor and sin in the First Baptist Church.

Those photos of grinning White girls and White boys
posing with a Black corpse their fathers and uncles
and neighbors had just created. We beyond all that.
Don't do no lynching no 'mo. Any more.

We got us a drone or two, which messes with what
we both knew by heart, Dad,
what all little boys know;
Everyone counts or no one counts.
How did we unlearn that? Growing Up.

Silhouettes of my ancestors, lets me think I know a thing or
two about you Dad. For a thousand years impressed
Catholics in Gaul and Albion, then Cranmer Anglicans Knox
Reformed Bunyan Baptists, into boats by choice or chance or
magistrate decree condemned to transport

Taylors and their married into New England with
expectations and designs
Taylors invented towns, killed and were killed
at the Wampanoag Fort in '76
that, boys, is 1676

Taylors invented schools, killed and were killed
as witches at Salem and in the fighting
around Dorchester Heights in '76
that, boys, is 1776.

Cooks and their married came on lower down
into Mr. Penn's forest and the Commonwealths below
With their children and their worked hard
sex-slave Colored

Their stand-up to decrees and pleas about not keeping
hold of their worked hard sex-slave Colored,
pass them around and down.
Thank you. Very much.

Dad was taken to watch a lynching.
Whole families invited.
Father, were you there?
Were you there when they crucified?
Oh, sometimes, daddy, it makes me tremble,
tremble
tremble.

Good Robert Coles My Zealous Interest Pricked

Good Robert Coles my zealous interest pricked
his Crisis Kids I read as sacred text
the Garden State in '70 was quick
to move the migrants on before their wrecked

and battered cars and lives could stop in town
the man-made Stream made men work dark to dim
was for their kind no place in Vineland found
the Migrant Stream was fine you see for them

Good Robert pointed gently to the souls
of children in a crisis not their choice
said specially for the poorest life unfolds
so quickly and is gone we'd best give voice

to small ones whose childhood is snatched away
by purposed, harsh and our cruel abuse
their dads and moms at hard labor all day
in fields that plied the nation's high produce

Good Robert not alone to sound the knell
to warn that children must be given more
than six inches of topsoil where some fell
and get six feet of earth 'til Heaven's door

swings open to receive them on that Day
when earth entire promised by Christ at last
theirs and dead Mom's and Dad's such deferred pay
like dust seems meager for a life-long fast

since food enough to live not theirs to tout
life on the Migrant Stream imparts slight hopes
for kids Good Robert chose to write about
for answers to these puzzles wisdom gropes

The other my pole star a stranger child
Unknown to me, but his reported de'f
and placement in the ground forced forward wild
and dismal thoughts his homeless folks bereft

they on the Stream, but Charlie left behind
in graved in Delaware forever lost
no locals would or could visit his kind
the migrant kid whose death a slighted cost

Some others offered up a hope with prayers
young Cesar and the workers plainly dressed
sang arm in arm then marched and tipped the chairs
made quake the agri-power in the west

came east they pitched a boycott had their say
don't buy the food and produce we would cut
and pack for decent wages they won't pay
this hopeful note got us out of the rut

of migrants streaming north from Floriday
the poorness of the boycott staff impressed
the prayers appealed to us who swing that way
with the UFW our hopes would crest

Our jump into this welcome stream secure
the Migrant Ministry blunted the edge
of poverty that volunteers endure
who aren't ordained before they reach the ledge

Chris Hartmire alter egoed Cesar's push
to trim the power of Calif agri-bis
but tempered with a charismatic rush
of love for us fools who signed up for this

new stream of work and play but industry
was why we'd come two thousand miles to be
told what to do and where to go each day
life that old song played in a grand new key

Unscrupulous in hope marked us as young
Incorrigible love seeks no amends
Nosotros Venceremos anthem sung
clasped happy hands bonded with new friends

Cesar the man in charge held all the reins
at first this pattern worked out to a tee
compellingly Chavez made wondrous gains
marked ordinary tasks with filigree

Disarming candor potion that confused
he'd pick his feet and talk of life long hate
for bosses who his grandad they'd abused
he'd set things right soon or maybe too late

The second tier of leaders brilliant too
LeRoy Jim Jerry Marshall none held back
from ceaseless duty exemplary few
were followed by an energetic pack

of bright and eager staffers not a few
could hold their own as dedicated men
and women who matched up quite well we knew
for workers' rights and union power its twin

We lived our little family at La Paz
solitary head in San Joaquin
the bastion and HDQ that was
or could have been my resting place I mean

I loved the winter crispness in that air
Union Pacific trills sweet spoke to me
of countless hobos riding to somewhere
to make a better life than they could see

I loved the desert harshness of that ground
the lack of color bright and varied seemed
the work was mediated by the sound
of children's laughter this place was my dream

but no, some crisis percolated all
save one or two no one would get to stay
the rest of us would quickly heed the call
to Arizona go or to L.A.

This rootless up and out tossed us about
and took the very meat right off the bone
of tireless then tired staff who came to doubt
had we turned not the tide but just the foam?

For us invited to live for the poor
the work beasts unrequited on this earth
a deep design good Cesar had in store
a commune or an Order he'd give birth

and turn it over to the Vatican
the autocrats of other people's souls
this leaves aside the strong woman or man
for whom a workers' union was the goal

Pues Cesar oye dinos what you mean
pull us away from Charlie Thomas' grave
the migrant boy whose death was so obscene
your fight's for wages or for souls to save?

And if I'd stayed behind to do what good
for kid like Charlie any case was dead
systemic powers had beat us where we stood
Might Good Robert as well just go unread

Cesar devout so quick to bend the knee
to court Mahoney's cynical good will
no clinic contraception he'd decree
but girlfriend gets the condom or the pill

US Labor power is grafted on
subject to ruin by legislative whim
rebellions in Europe guard gains hard won
since 1848 those ranks have thinned

Sacramento, a sacrament became
long pilgrimage of talent, money too
made sense to fix this tiresome dance for gain
stick labor law with constitution glue

It did not work for reasons that apply
to other propositions we deride
but Cesar thought to win was as to try
and lose meant rot was buried deep inside

Purged those kids a deed surely ironic
the very ones whose work back in the day
had made the union's label iconic
were marched out of La Paz sent on their way

Like me some kept our heads we kept them low
but this is not the mission of the brave
righteous we self-envisioned long ago
we came to help the workers not self-save

Not one thought but a thousand fill each hour
a busy forward looking plan was urged
at bay kept somber musings from power
to notify the purger bro you're purged

Sublime vision our noon devil became
LeRoy long gone Jim Eliseo too
postulants from La Paz increasing lame
the worst of it so many now too few

My mentor Chris moved to the fortress high
our shattered ranks to me looked for a sign
expected All's well from me but a sigh
I offered them before up and resign

All faithful were we and all traitors too
In solitude each measures down the love
the balance once expended well you're through
You're strangers now who once worked hand in glove

Of my one thousand thoughts cascade each hour
one troubles me more than the last or first
my opt for Califa to fight the Powers
was that my best decision or my worst?

Together yoked we labored how we worked
In the deepening sunset sharpness lost
Recall no task too tiresome to be shirked
or questions asked but still there comes the cost

Is life tainted if you intend for good?
Severe inquiry dare not pose the grave
fanatic who will kill you if he could
pray weeping o'er your corpse whose soul he'd save

Your blind allegiance tolls on you its cost
won't be shifted to the one who beckoned
we answered then now looking back have lost
the lifetime we better might have reckoned

Life unobstructed if the backward look
brings out a chorus dear whose spectral aire
praises our efforts inscribed in the book
of small deeds, as no large are written there?

Joe Qualey's Watch in My Sock Drawer

Sugar, you want Joe Qualey's watch?

Aunt Carrie shouted at me from maybe three feet away.
Carrie always talked like you were hard of hearing, no matter
the subject, no matter, in this case,
she was talking about suicide.

I said sure, so she handed it to me,
along with her Joe Qualey story.

Roaring 20's Joe Qualey drowned himself in a swimming pool
out on Long Island, leaving Ethel to explain it all to their two
young sons, or maybe let them figure out their dad had killed
himself after their mother's money had run out.

Under the circumstances, easy to see why Ethel had no
interest in the watch. It probably went into a box, if Dorland
and Carrie had to go to New York and help Ethel
deal with things after the death.

The other day, I got out Joe Qualey's watch. Its not Joe's.
Looks like it's his father-in-law's. Old man Dorland's money
went probably to buy that or any watch.

The old man's watch has gotten into my sock drawer and
kicked out Joe's watch. At least that's what I think.
Time will tell.

Por David Urias - Asesinado
a los diecinueve años de edad
Palo Bonito, Cabañas, El Salvador
29 junio 2012

El dió con senderos conocidos
Mostraba confianza su paso
Ilusiones reales no presumidas
Varonil su aspecto leve acaso

Dió David con senda familiar
Bajaba en parada habitual
Jamás piensa en sangre bautizar
Ir a hogar humilde y natal

Proyectos bien de paz y comunal
Guardaba en su mente inocente
Camina alegre pero el Mal
lo rodea atrás y en el frente

Lastimaron al muchacho sin perdón
También falta razón a perdonar
Libre de actos malos, fue el don
a todos; pues su meta fue amar

David! Quitarte todo! Bien feo!
al comienzo de tu mero apogeo

For David Urias - Murdered
At Nineteen Years of Age
Palo Bonito, Cabañas, El Salvador
June 29 2012

He followed paths well worn and well known
His footfall ever confident and sure
His dreams though not pretentious nor full grown
His manly aspect gentle, immature

He walked the ways of neighbors gone before
His journey home habitual, routine
They laid in wait to baptize him in gore
No more his features by his mother seen

His simple plans were peaceful, made for all
Communal good, his grand intended goal
Guided by pleasant thoughts before the gall
of bitter, blinded hatred his life-gift stole

They hurt this boy without reason, hate-filled
and lacking too, a pretext for their rage
free of the slightest malice, he was killed
this gift of love was driven from life's stage

David, oh, your precious life is spent
Just as you began your grand ascent

Ataduras

Sentado cómodo en mi sillón
Mirando a mis perritos que no saben
Que a David el otro día lo mataron
El na' mas caminaba a casa de su Mami
Ella con el chucho esperando al cipote,
tampoco sabía el chucho que David está muerto ya
y que al chucho mismo lo matarán,
segundo aviso que te largues de aquí
quita cualquier pendejada que no les guste

Strings Attached

Sitting there in comfortable clothes
looking at my two dogs who don't know
David was murdered the other day
walking to his home where his mother
waited for him with her dog who also
did not know David was already dead
and also would be killed
a second message to get the Hell out of there
stop with whatever bullshit it is they don't like.

David, Quiero Acuñar Una Moneda

David, quiero acuñar una moneda
con una cara en un lado
Por otro
una lágrima
David

David, I Want to Mint a Coin

David, I want to mint a coin
with a face on one side
On the other
a tear
David

En las Películas

Dos boletos. Uno por cada niño.
Ellos entran a las tinieblas, donde residen extraños.
Sus pasos acelerados, sus inclinaciones hacia delante
Anticipan deleites venideros.
No más.
Con chirridos suaves, cara hacia la oscuridad
Esperan diversiones.
No más.

Saben que sus padres están divididos,
Ya no viven en un mismo lugar.
Como polluelos en nido alto, crecen sus hambres
con creciente conciencia de que la figura protector
no aparece desde hace tiempo,
Aprenderán que la oscuridad trae
aparte de los placeres.
No más.

At the Movies

Two tickets, one per child.
They walk into shadows peopled by strangers.
His quickened step, her forward lean
Anticipate pleasures to come.
Nothing more.
Softly chirping, heading toward that darkness
They expect only to be entertained.
Nothing more.

They know their parents are divided
No longer living in one place together.
Like chicks in a high nest, whose rising hungers
match a new awareness that the protector
has not appeared in a while,
They will learn that darkness brings
other than pleasures.
Nothing more.

Contronym Promesa

Acumulación de promesas incumplidas
Como piedra de afilar
ha formado el cuchillo
por su trabajo.

El cuchillo ha escindido dos
que había prometido
escindir
uno al otro.

Contronym Promise

Accretion of broken promises,
Like a whetstone
has fashioned the cleaver
for its work.

The cleaver has cleaved two
who had promised
to cleave
to each other.

Fearless Lieder

Not young, Johannes yet wrote two a day
Discoverer, no, creator of worlds
Scratched out the notes, paced, stranger to dismay
We feel awed by such certainty unfurled

So listen, strain to catch the deeper thought
Johannes, older, still keeps up the pace
His muse, amused, since Brahms thinks she's been caught
Naked, she blows kisses against his face

February 12, 1809

Abe Lincoln first then Charles Darwin appears
Evolved fast in our midst from spheres unseen
Abe dropped his axe to stem the nation's tears
Concealed his thoughts balked Charlie not demean
The eye of faith blind to the facts he'd seen

Abe held that peoples one people can be
Blood met with blood of those who disagree
His critics charged he'd swung down from a tree
We all did proved Charles scientifically
Both boys select of us naturally

Genealogy Chorus

In the ground these hundreds years
Left few hints your joys and tears
Some you rich some in arrears
I know you

Some you brave some felled by fear
Some despised and some were dear
You in living ken appear
I know you

All you died been dead so long
Picked out all you from the throng
Join you soon now won't be long
I know you

Indian Summer Maryland, 2013

- For PJ and Vicky -

The parking lot was full and so the pews.
You walk together into smiles, old friends.
Hymns, promises, prayers, words of justice, grace.
Applause. You kiss, retreat, though not so far.

Your twelve past warming, windy summers come,
but this Summer finds sound legal effect.
The aged father, aided in, approves.
The young mother, for her infant, approves.

Rood relic, cousin to that cruciate post,
that ancient hemic beam, approves let be.
A gentle murmur through bleached leaves approves
departed, present Indian Summerers.

KY Grand Prix c. 1850

Ask yourself and be honest.
Juat what would you have done different?
She's fourteen, wearing hardly a stitch.
Milking the cow, feeding the mule.
Barefoot. Hitching up that potato sack of a dress.
You know there's nothing under.
Accept her flesh.

Not a thing in the world anyone can say or do.
Not a measly thing.
She's fourteen, she been looking at you, must have.
She does not smile but she does not frown.
She looks away, an invitation, gotta be.
Who cares anyway? Not a measly thing.
Billy Dick did it in his time. He told me all about it.

You walk up behind, take a'hold.
She drops the handful of feed.
Chickens come a running. Pecking.
Be silly stand there now all them chickens.
You move your hand to the back of her neck
Walk her into the woods
That spot you already had in mind.

Jerk that sack right off her.
Throw it on the ground.
Make her lie down on it.
Not a stitch just like you knew.
You want her to smile.
You don't care if she smile.
You wan'a be the first.

I Like the GPS

I like the GPS recalculate
the automatic digital one eye
resets itself so guided won't be late
the mindlessly directed such as I

My own recalculations are a guess
a throw against uncertainties which come
like waves up on my beach and the piled mess
of projects plans proposals the sad sum

of efforts stalled forgotten botched mislaid
recalculations due when aged frames
no longer can support the vows we made
to self, others, to win at the great game

From birth to death one lesson muddles fate
your destination is . . . recalculate

Mechanics of the Cycle, Hopes Quickened

Mechanics of the cycle, hopes quickened
Warm longer days, sure signs that God has blest
Ourselves above the stupefying rest
Pup gnaws the carcass young Spring had sickened.

Today Is Election Day

Gentle drill of rain bowing the green blades
They genuflect, quick rising, kneel again
The swallow trills her poll; the choice is made
to stay for now in the cathedral glen

Mowing the Grass, 1958

Small blades of grass fly high like volunteers
who jump quick to the front in vernal clash.
Fresh cuttings smell of damp soft evening cheer.
Whur of the blades, like furious teeth, gnash.

Dad pushed that mower across the yard, again.
He lost his pastorate that year. In fact
he quit. He could not preach to them of sin
or heaven's promises or hell's fast track.

Those heedless jowled fools whose friend he'd been.
They would not raise his pay, said he had cash.
Weeds, dandelions, men reduced again
To cosmic elements by timely slash.

Dad cut that green grass down by God to size
then burned the sermons he'd come to despise.

Milton Visita al Galileo Condenado

Ojos crispados, en Florencia, Milton
Toca, entra, ve lo que ignoran los demás
Il Signore ciego sonríe, es el hijo.
Pide besos paternales en la faz.

"Ves bien, cuerpos celestes, gran Señor"
- "Tus poemas, contraparte, rimador."
"Que no te toque el torp' Inquisidor!"
- "Artes no agotan, artista empuj' el flor."

Al partir, cortó rosa, sonrió.
"Encuentro bien dulce se recordó"
- "Después escribes, hijo, que se vió.
"Venir la oscuridad, no s'anticipó."

Juan e il Signore visión perder.
El ojo dentro derrot' anochecer.

Milton Visits the Condemned Galileo

With twitching eyes, in Florence, raps young John
Admitted, he sees well what some do miss
The blind *Signore* smiles as if a son
Appears now to receive a father's kiss

'Your works give Heaven's parts their truest place'
- 'May thou become my counterpart in rhyme'
'May wound ye not Inquisitor's disgrace'
- 'Unbounded arts, though artists bound in time'

Departing, young John cut a rose and smiled
'This sweet encounter long shall be recalled'
- 'Read now, son, later write what you have styled
- 'The coming darkness will not be forestalled.'

Both John and *il Signore* lost their sight
The mind's eye sees into the dimmest night.

Oso Mi Papá

Curioso, amoroso, chistoso
Hosco, ojeroso, pavoroso

Provechoso, silencioso, piadoso
Furioso, rabioso, ruidoso

Majestuoso, meticuloso, talentoso
quisquilloso, riguroso, doloroso

Misericordioso, amistoso, aventuroso
Escabroso, odioso, temeroso

Dichoso, generoso, decoroso
Vigoroso, peligroso, espantoso

My Dad the Bear

Funny, loving, humorous
Sullen, haggard, creepy

Helpful, quiet, pious
Furious, rabid, noisy

Majestic, meticulous, accomplished
Fussy, rigorous, distressing

Gracious, friendly, adventurous
Rough, hateful, fearsome

Happy, generous, dignified
Robust, dangerous, frightening

Pastoral Bandwidth

The old man never spoke
Never moved from his bed
A stretched out farmer
Dying in an 1820's farmhouse

Was it a stroke?
Was he tired right down to the ground?
Did he believe his dying room already held
all the words that would fit?

91, in Hospice

Awake, she eats with unexpected haste
Hands flying over the tray spilling nothing

Coffee's stone cold, she says to the room
Ignoring the gloved hand caressing her hair

Philosophy of Broken Toys

We all do it. Look back at young years through gauze
When we were held in strong arms,
Protected by large hands
When we knew the future would be grand for us
Like our bedroom, our backyard
When all the music we heard was true.

The forties and fifties was my gauze time
Running in warmth, walking in snow
Putting miles, hills, between pre-me and
The sorrows of some and to come.
When Doris Day, Ernie Ford, Perry Como, Patti Page
were philosophers.
When Ike was the father and we did not yet know
to hate Nixon, given to us by our neglectful dad,
an already broken and jagged toy.

Mother, father, our children, call up their own
gauze times, when they were held in strong arms and hands,
when the future would be grand and their toys, like ours,
were not observed as already broken
When their music. like ours, made by philosophers,
Vallee, Marley, was true.

Nov 2012, Prayer for the Archbishop
(Offered During the Two-Minute Timeout)

I don't think the Cosmic Christ was half-assed
or a simpleton, or a my way or the highway
type of guy.

Although I could be wrong about that last item
if not about all three items and all other items
for that matter.

But I will tell you this,
more chips?
a guy who will lie right into a microphone,
thanks,

is not the type of guy you can afford to have
making life and death decisions
over your sorry
ass.

Raising funds for a dead boy's family
(at a church in baltimore county maryland)

Out of the blue, sometimes, we flat out burst into tears
Don't we?
May as well just admit it 'cause it's true.
Right there, for no reason at all.

The receptionist said through the speaker box next to the
locked door, just leave what you have on the ground
she said,
Someone will come and pick it up.
Right there. On the ground.

She didn't know that David was standing there
with no head
since they crushed it and left his body
where his mother would find him.
Right there, for no reason at all.

David's mom was there too, wondering
what was I going to do now.
David's sisters were standing a little ways off,
watching.
Right there, for no reason at all.

I love you
It's no big deal
I'm past all that
I didn't mean it
You asked for it
Do what you like
With all my heart
Let's just start over
It won't happen again
Tell me what you think
We are in this together
It doesn't matter to me
Let me run this by you
That's not what I mean
That's not what I meant
It's not about the money
You can tell me anything
You can tell me everything
I would never do that to you
Nothing can come between us
You know me better than that
The kids come first, like always
You have my complete support
Don't know what came over me
That's the most important thing
He doesn't mean anything to me
Let's try it and see what happens
She doesn't mean anything to me
I would never hold that against you

Ripped Messiah

Easter reminds us we will stand again
Anastasia - dance card of the young
We wrinkled can't relate or recall when
with brawn we pulled up from the bottom rung

Enough we don't fall down. Now take your pills.
Live it all again? No fond desire.
What if the crucified on Calvary's Hill
An old dude, carpenter 'fore gospel fire

Made him shake his cane at those righteous swells
they killed him, leaving grandma, sad grandkids
weeping at his cross. Would sedate church bells
salute codger-messiah on the skids?

The Savior of the World he best be ripped
with tats, tall mohawk, ring in those big lips.

Short Order

The spike hair corner cook slides through his tasks
The diners 'lone or paired, shout choice like darts
Complying Cookie moves to meet their asks
Slight shoulder hutch binds suffering to his arts

Spring Preyers

Bold early Spring promises tint and hue
as yet unseen. Dull browns still rule our wood.
Debris of stick and decay will renew
Dry brittle leaves where rhododendrons stood.

We gather ourselves and the tools as well
stashed over from last summer's warm assaults.
New chirp and rustle each is Nature's tell
for winning cards she'll lay on winter faults.

Ourselves no longer hide the winding up
of cycles seen without and felt within.
We ask in vain like Jesus, take the cup
away. Can't we, like geia, start again?

Come Spring! Bring hints of yellow, green and red!
Slow carrion hunters descending overhead.

Simulacra

The restless simulacra in my mind,
The piquant and horrific mix and meet.
Kaleidoscopic images unwind,
Make loves of losses, victories defeat.

With slight adjustments, just the merest twist,
My brain creates the past I would review.
The sum of spent events comes down to this:
What's said and done I constantly renew.

Kaleidoscopic colors can enchant,
The reds, the greens, the yellows do enthrall.
More somber hues, though true, I can recant,
Since truth is true when willingly recalled.

The present from the past - a common view.
Our memories we invent - more likely true.

Te Mataron, David, Por Que?

David, te quitaron tus mañanas
tu temor, tu bravura, tu suerte
tus arrugas merecidas, tus ganas
tu rostro, tus ayeres, tu muerte

de anciano digno y honrado
por tu mujer, tus niños, tus nietos
alivios por tu tiempo largo
por voluntad bien sutil de Dios

Te quitaron tus sueños propios
tus ilusiones compartidas
tus días letargos y únicos
Vos! Tus tristezas, tus alegrías.

No te queda ni lo que has sido
transiente chispa frente el olvido

David - Why Did They Murder You?

David, your tomorrows they stole entire
With your fears, your cockiness, your trying
your latent wrinkles, your private desires
your presence, your past, your distant dying

As one grown ancient, honored, dignified
touched by a wife, by kids, grandchildren, too
relieved after a long, well measured ride
in God's too subtle will, for me and you

They took away David your every muse
Your hopes some private, some with others shared
Your days lethargic, or unique, confused
Your sadnesses, your ecstasies, none spared

Nothing remains, not even what you'd been
a transient spark between oblivions

On Not Questioning My Grandmother

Now, questions break like spray in grand cascade.
How could they not? Blanche died before I asked
Of James and Arabelle, the pair who made
Her. Then, while young, my declarations fast.

Now, old, slow, would give years to hear her voice.
Were your folks sweet to you, dear Blanche? I'd say.
When you picked Cecil, they approve your choice?
Your Pa he wore the Blue, Cec's dad the Gray.

When 'Belle your Mom died you blame God or fate?
You go with Cecil just to get away?
You knew James' mother? Simple not ornate.
At least the one picture we have would say.

Now, drenched in ignorant old age, I fret,
Loosed from this moil, might I get answers yet?

When She was Twenty-four and I Was

Soft beauty, straighted by propriety
At twenty-four, her scent my universe
We grew apart, but not unhappily
I learned from her firm striving, then the curse

Of gathered space and time made final end
Of days and nights we shared. So soon I left
Returned from time to time, would rarely send
A note, detect slight sense she felt bereft

First bed we shared, remotest memory
For crowded in my life those dear enlarged
Souls with their own right, good, sure claims on me.
Advanced in years she hinted I be charged

With tasks unknown when she was twenty-four
In her last bed, inhale Mother once more

www.ingramcontent.com/pod-product-compliance
Lightning Source LLC
Chambersburg PA
CBHW072039060426
42449CB00010BA/2357